WELL, THIS IS ME

WELL, THIS IS ME

A cartoon collection from the *New Yorker's*

ASHER PERLMAN

Andrews McMeel
PUBLISHING®

Andrews McMeel Publishing
a division of Andrews McMeel Universal
1130 Walnut Street, Kansas City, Missouri 64106

www.andrewsmcmeel.com

Comics on pages 17, 78, 83, 85, 87, 88, 100, 101, 112, 165, and 167 originally appeared in the *New Yorker*.

24 25 26 27 28 VEP 10 9 8 7 6 5 4 3

ISBN: 978-1-5248-9205-0

Library of Congress Control Number: 2023950813

Editor: Patty Rice
Art Director: Holly Swayne
Production Editor: Elizabeth A. Garcia
Production Manager: Chadd Keim

ATTENTION: SCHOOLS AND BUSINESSES
Andrews McMeel books are available at quantity discounts with bulk purchase for educational, business, or sales promotional use. For information, please e-mail the Andrews McMeel Publishing Special Sales Department: sales@amuniversal.com.

This book is dedicated to all parents who encourage their children to pursue creativity, but especially mine: Rachel and Steve Perlman.

And to Nikki.

CONTENTS

INTRODUCTION

So, how did you get into comedy?

Well, the modern human brain hasn't really changed in the last 35,000 years, which means the one in my head is identical to what you would find in the skulls of my prehistoric ancestors.

At that time, people lived in small, close-knit tribes in which social approval was essential to survival.

Because if you were kicked out of the group, you would actually die.

Now we live in cities of millions, with the internet giving us theoretical access to billions, a number which is literally unfathomable.

All of that means that our reasonable, inherent desire to be liked by our immediate circle has now morphed into the perverse, unattainable goal of receiving everyone's love at all times forever.

I guess I've just always
loved making people laugh.

WELL, THIS IS WORK

"Over the next three hours, I will show you how to stretch 30 minutes of information across three hours."

"Welcome to Sal's Pizza and Ceiling Fans."

"My weekend was pretty good. I didn't accomplish the one thing
I was supposed to, but at least I thought about it the whole time
so everything fun I did instead was ruined."

"For your final labour, you must open this pistachio that doesn't already have a little slit in its shell."

"Oh great, the pervert's back."

"I'm Matthew's dad, and I _also_ make more and work less than Ms. Hudson."

"And the person who is about to experience a sudden dopamine rush followed quickly by the realization that their life is unchanged, still empty, is . . ."

"*We, the jury, find the defendant.*"

"You have the right to remain silent, but fair warning: I'm super uncomfortable with silence and will fill it with increasingly personal stories that I'll regret sharing later."

"*The good news is, we caught it early enough to operate.
The bad news is, I always put things off to the last minute.*"

"I can't hear yoooouuu!"

"If I'm going to become the best exterminator in town,
I need to practice."

"Have you tried licking it for hours?"

"*Our prices range from unaffordable to frankly deranged.*"

"We used to use that stuff, but now we just tell people
that we heard juicy gossip that we can't share."

"Prices are marked, but the real cost is enduring
my undivided attention while you browse."

"It's not broken, but just to be safe, I say we pull it out and bury it in the backyard."

"I try to tell a story with my art."

"The surgery is major and the recovery excruciating,
but at least reinjury is all but certain."

"Your first assignment is to make a monthly budget for
a middle-aged man with $100K in loans, trying to raise
two kids on an adjunct professor's salary."

"We offer health insurance as well as a stressful,
sedentary existence that guarantees you'll need it."

"Oh fuck yes. Let's make these fuckers live for-fucking-ever."

"The breakfast is free, unless you count the cost of thinking you're dining alone only to be joined by a colleague who is also staying at the hotel."

"Off with his head! On with a new head!
Let the great experiment begin!"

"Of course, the real enemy is negative self-talk."

"*We want you to know that the leadership team is always open to any and all positive feedback.*"

"*I mean, I __can__ throw it a third time.*"

"I think I know the problem: you have a thousand dollars
that I want."

"Give us your money, your jewelry, and, if you happen to have one, a bandana for Bart here."

"You're actually quite lucky. Most professors wouldn't step up like this when a model called out sick."

"You'll be hearing from my attorney! Not because I'm taking legal action but because he thinks you're cute and I gave him your number. It was unprofessional and an invasion of privacy. I'm sorry!"

41

"Before you bust me for counterfeiting, perhaps you'd like to meet my good friend Warren G. Harding."

"*Don't worry. Agent Harris here is the best there is at hiding wires.*"

"*Ladies and gentlemen, I don't know anything more than you do.
My authority is an illusion. The universe is chaos.
We should begin moving shortly.*"

"Now that you're technically awake but still totally out of it, let's go over important post-care instructions you need to follow closely or else you die."

"No, Goldstein, I don't think we should 'try a silly one.'"

"Do you know why I pulled you over? Because I forgot."

asher

"*Making my initial incision.*"

"*I've always struggled with accepting praise.*"

"All hail Sir 'Oops That's Sharp.'"

"It went triple platinum, but I was hoping it would stop at gold."

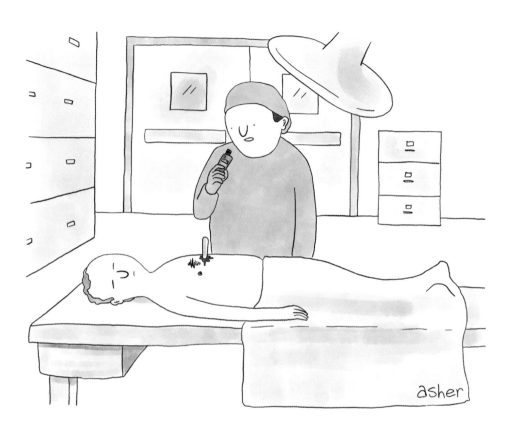

"Cause of death appears to be me freaking out and stabbing him in the chest after he woke up on the table having been mistakenly diagnosed as dead."

"Actually, the mayor would like to cut the cord."

"*You may approach the bench.*"

"*Did I overhear that someone in here is naughty?*"

"*Just make it fast—oh god.*"

"Thanks, yeah, they're beautiful. The only downside is that I'm super allergic, so I keep breaking out into sudden, uncontrollable sneezing fits."

"We opened 15 minutes ago, so we're running two hours behind."

WELL, THIS IS PLAY

"Question one: how can you stay up this late drinking on a Tuesday?"

"Well, I'd love to keep talking to you, a true friend who makes me feel appreciated and wholly accepted, but I just spotted an aloof acquaintance whose approval I could desperately seek."

"Let's get reeeaady to quueesstion the ethiiiics of waaatching thiiiis."

"*Now sit back, relax, and learn the hard way that the symphony is more the kind of thing you <u>want</u> to like.*"

"Well, I'm gonna take off, unless you bully me into having 'just one more' because for some reason you want to hang out with someone who would rather be home."

"We used to have group sex, but this is way more intimate."

"Before you leave for vacation, let me send you a painstaking list of recommendations to ignore."

"Can you use it in a sentence, or, if you're up for it,
a dazzling song?"

"While our partners are in the bathroom, would you prefer awkward small talk or awkward silence?"

"If you're looking for life advice, my suggestion is that you make the same decisions I made so that I feel validated in mine."

"*You guys each need a vital organ? Yeah, basically same:
I kinda hate my personality.*"

"Actually, we're fraternal."

*"For my final feat, I will move to New York City
without rich parents."*

"*To throw the first pitch, please welcome some guy you're all about to google.*"

"Ring it again. I bet he's hiding under the bed."

"*For my first trick, I'll show you how I saved $175 by being the magician at my own daughter's birthday party even though my wife made me promise I wouldn't do that.*"

"*Ladies and gentlemen, this is your captain speaking,
and this is your captain siiinnngiiinnng.*"

"You each have 30 minutes and a particularly
extroverted spouse. Go!"

"Have you heard the one about the dad who forgot the supplies for s'mores and didn't know how to break it to the children?"

"You wanna take this o-u-t-s-i-d-e?"

"I dooon't know this sooonngg. I'm just heeeerree with my
dauuughter and her friiiieeeends."

"It's either this or ask you to repeat yourself a third time."

"*We will now begin boarding Group 2 and anyone from Group 3 or 4 bold enough to try.*"

"Which one is yours?"

"I have to get up early, so I'm gonna go to bed now and lie there wide awake until I would normally go to bed."

"*Sorry if there's sand back there. I went to the beach once ten years ago.*"

"*Thank you! Now, behold, as I turn 'a week tops'
into three goddamn months!*"

"Oh god, he's going for the jukebox!"

"When we agreed to take turns with the radio, nobody stipulated that I couldn't use mine on the 54-hour audiobook of David McCullough's masterful Harry Truman biography."

"Instead of blowing money on food at the gate, I packed us some snacks that taste bad so we still end up blowing money on food at the gate."

"Behold! As I try to live with what I've done, who I've become."

"The last time I went this long without drinking enough water was every day of my life."

*"Think about it: we only come here once a year,
but if we became members, we could feel more guilty about that."*

"And that's why every kid with a single mom should tell her that there's nothing sexier than a puppeteer."

"Sailing is so relaxing. Just us, the open sea,
and a literal endless succession of little tasks."

"I find that belonging to a CSA is the most effective way to throw away a box of rotten vegetables every week."

"It doesn't matter how valuable the manuscript
is to _you_, Charles."

"*Do you have any true-crime podcasts?*"

"*If I knew it was gonna be this slow, I would have waited to say goodbye.*"

INTERLUDE

So, how did you decide on cartooning?

I didn't.

In fact, I wouldn't say that I've "chosen" to do anything in my career.

I knew early on that I wanted to work in comedy, but this industry is so fickle and out of anyone's control that opportunities arise seemingly at random, and all you can do is let chance guide you and see where you end up. In that sense, every "choice" I've made has really just been the byproduct of chaos and path dependency.

IN ONE MILE, AUDITION FOR BEER COM- MERCIAL

Beyond that, as a collection of matter, my entire existence is nothing more than a series of physical processes following cosmic rules that date all the way back to the Big Bang.

Toss in a pinch of randomness, and I'm really a mere witness to my decisions, an external observer watching myself with wonder and confusion.

I kind of regret asking.

If it helps, you didn't have a choice.

WELL, THIS IS LOVE

"You also <u>may</u> kiss me, but no pressure."

"I just don't think I want kids."

"But we just got here."

"I want to do one of those fun fantasies where we go to a hotel bar and pretend to be strangers, and you try to pick me up, but I think you're disgusting and run away with the bartender, who is very strong and not at all like you, and the strong bartender and I start a new life together, and I never see you again."

"*Keep in mind that, by the day of the wedding,
I plan on being jacked.*"

"I love you more than you'll ever know because I'm a lousy communicator and struggle with being vulnerable."

"*From the gentleman at the end of the bar.*"

"*I need a verbal yes.*"

"Dearly beloved, we are gathered here today to collectively wonder if Nicole could have done better."

"You don't think I respect your privacy??"

"Breakups are hard, but chin up, buddy. I just saw a sign
that said it's our season."

"Aw, look at how happy we were pretending to be
for this picture."

"What do you mean you're having an affair with the pool boy?"

"It's actually a cute story: we both have pretty devastating
unresolved attachment issues."

"*Honey, get the bat.*"

"*This apartment ain't big enough for the both of us.*"

*"Good luck coming up with your 10th commandment, honey.
I'm heading out to dinner with the neighbor."*

"That's odd. The apology I relentlessly bullied you
into giving me doesn't feel quite sincere."

asher

"Dinner will be ready as soon as I've dirtied every dish in the kitchen."

"*Of course this is devastating, but I'm also always a little relieved when someone cancels plans last minute.*"

"But if I'm not his father, who is?"

"Under 'Grounds for divorce,' you just wrote,
'Replying to, "I hate the way I look in that picture,"
with, "But that's how you look."'"

"Of course I'm upset that you're having an affair, but I'm more just impressed that you have the energy to pull it off."

"Two lines means we're going to have a cold
twice a month for six years."

WELL, THIS IS LIFE

"If it helps, you're also insignificant from a non-cosmic perspective."

"Okay, I think I finally feel financially stable enough to have a child."

"The special tonight is vomit. Vomit straight from my mouth."

"If you think asking, 'What's the worst that could happen?'
is comforting, you clearly underestimate my ability to
imagine bad things."

"Aw, Gavin's dreaming that he's running."

"Now that you've defended your dissertation,
your parents here would like you to defend your decision
to get a PhD in philosophy."

"No, thanks. I hate interacting with strangers."

"I'll sleep when I'm dead or 20 minutes into any movie."

"Sometimes I worry that I've peaked creatively."

"I <u>am</u> living in the moment. It's just one from yesterday when I said something stupid."

"You don't need to do that little flourish <u>every</u> time I emerge."

*"I'm living each day like it's my last:
demented, in bed, dwelling on my mistakes."*

"Please remove your shoes, realize you forgot to wear socks, accept your fate, and make peace with your god."

"It's like I always say: life is too nuanced for anything to be generally true enough to always say."

"*Shoot, I know I came in here for a reason.*"

"And this machine's job is to beep every time
you're about to fall asleep."

"I lost your college fund in a game of roulette, but before you get upset, know that it was mathematically a better investment."

"I take this pill to help me sleep a full eight hours and then be utterly useless for the following 12."

"*Well, the most valuable thing I can give you is my time.*"

"Sorry, I really don't know how to take a compliment."

"Just out of curiosity, how many more kids did you tell that your dad could beat up their dad?"

"Sorry, I just loaded up all the machines, but don't worry:
I'll return to take out my laundry the second you've given up
waiting and started removing armfuls of my wet underwear."

"If you are watching this, it means that I am dead. Either that or I got impatient and wanted to see your reaction."

"In this particular case, I think life might be at least somewhat about the destination."

"I hear someone here likes The Spider Man . . ."

"Sorry, but I just had an idea, and if I don't write it down now,
I won't be able to read it in the morning and realize it's insane."

"*I could tell you precisely what's wrong, but my business model kinda depends on dragging it out for years.*"

"Young MacDonald had a dream."

asher

"Sorry, I laugh when I'm uncomfortable and watching a funny video on my phone."

"*Due to extreme curiosity, the plane is being redirected to a nearby airport.*"

"*You can't do that, Scott—this is Chicago.*"

"He looks like he's sleeping."

"I'm gonna make him an offer he could refuse
but won't because he's afraid of conflict."

"Allll cleeeeaar. Sleeeeeep nowww, my deliccciousss sonnn."

"*Car crash, eh? Yeah, basically same: I stood up weird.*"

"It may feel like everyone is thinking about you, but the truth is they're far too busy worrying about themselves, Dan."

"They say you shouldn't <u>speak</u> ill of the dead."

"When traffic is bad, I sound my horn. That way, the traffic is bad but also loud."

"How do I safely dispose of these batteries?"

"High angle! High angle!"

"You are not the father! No, for that is a title you must earn.
You are, however, the biological dad."

"*Well, now I just want to know the purpose of the <u>after</u>life.*"

EPILOGUE

It's clear that you're afraid of giving an honest, personal answer, so you couch everything in either a joke or an objective statement about the universe.

Actually, I was just going to say that cartooning is truly my favorite thing to do, that it helps me untangle the world and to express myself, and that I've always wanted to have a compilation of my own like the ones I read as a kid.

Okay, fine. I was going to say that other stuff.

I know.

ACKNOWLEDGMENTS

They say it takes a village, but, in my case, it was more like a major metropolitan area.

To Nikki Cimoch, you are my first reader, my final editor, and my forever love. I'm grateful that you have such a high tolerance for hearing, "Do you get this?"

To my family—Rachel, Steve, Jacob, Reuven, Ondrea, and Erin—I can't express in words how much you mean to me, but I promise to never stop trying. Mom, I would be nowhere without your ferocious support and guidance. Pop, your early art lessons and passion for cartooning set me on this path. Jake, you're a true inspiration to me, artistically and personally. And Reuv, my comedic sensibility was forged in the fire of our conversations. Thanks for being my wombmate.

To my book agent, Alex Rice, as well as my non-book agents, Andy Elkin, Jacquie Katz, and Ally Shuster, I say with no hyperbole that this book wouldn't exist without you. Thank you for being my champions from the jump.

To everyone at Andrews McMeel, but especially Patty Rice: As a child of the '90s, I was effectively co-parented by your book catalog. It means so much to be a part of this family alongside my heroes.

To my *New Yorker* editor, Emma Allen: No one's email address in my inbox floods my brain with more dopamine. I'm forever grateful to you.

To Stephen Colbert, Tom Purcell, and Jordan Klepper: Thank you for gifting me the opportunity to work in television. My fingers ache from the number of times I've pinched myself.

Thank you to my friends who gave feedback without which this book would be immeasurably worse: Lily Ball, Delmonte Bent, Michelle Bisson, River Clegg, Chelsea Davison, Chelsea Devantez, Ariel Dumas, Tim Dunn, Ivan Ehlers, Django Gold, Blythe Haaga, Mark Johnson, Ryan Jones, Jason Adam Katzenstein, Amy Kurzweil, Suerynn Lee, Brendan Loper, Navied Mahdavian, Jeremy Nguyen, Tyler Parker, Vince Portacci, Molly Rugg, John Sabine, Sofia Warren, and Zach Zimmerman.

Special shout-out to Steve Waltien and Eliana Kwartler, who combed through hundreds of cartoons to help with the initial pass. Your discerning eyes are invaluable and should be studied for science.

Finally, if you're someone who should be on this list and isn't, please know it was a mistake and that you're in good company—I deliberately didn't include Ellis Rosen, whose contributions were incalculable, just to make you feel better.